RECOVERING FROM DIVORCE

PARTICIPANT GUIDE

VINCE FRESE

Divorced Catholic Publishing

www.divorcedcatholic.com

CONTENTS

Welcome --5

Contents of the Participant Kit -----------------------------------9

How to Use the Participant Kit -----------------------------------11

Tapping Into Your Catholic Faith --------------------------------15

The P-R-A-Y Method ---31

Participating in a Group ---49

Recovering from Divorce Sessions --------------------------------55

WELCOME

Something tells me that you never thought you would ever buy something titled *Recovering from Divorce*. Well, I never thought I would ever create any program, let alone a program to help Catholics recover from divorce. So, there, we're even. :-)

What you hold in your hands is the collective wisdom, teaching, and power of the Catholic Church. My role was simply to compile it in a format that is easy to understand and use. When I went through my divorce over fifteen years ago, there was nothing available in my parish (or archdiocese) to help me — I was on my own.

It took me about five years of fumbling around in my faith, digging for the truth, working through many misconceptions, and making many mistakes (a nice way of saying I was sinning a lot), before I had a good understanding of what it meant to be divorced and Catholic.

In all of that fumbling, digging, and making mistakes, something miraculous happened: I was healed from the wounds of my divorce. As a result, I learned something critical to my recovery: the Catholic Church has all the answers I was looking for. Better still, it contained everything I needed to fully recover from my divorce and be restored to the fullness of life.

I took everything I learned and created the *Recovering from Divorce Program*. By God's grace, He allowed me to suffer through my divorce, and be healed by my faith in Him, so I can share that with you. As a result, hopefully, you won't have to struggle and thrash around as much as I did. You can learn from me and get on track to fully recovering from your divorce.

The *Recovering from Divorce Program* is a thirteen session program. While I would love to tell you that by using this program you can fully recover from your divorce in three months, I think that would be unrealistic. Certainly, Our Lord can heal you in an instant if He so desires. In His great wisdom He realizes that humans need time to learn, change, and heal. The Program gets you started on that path and, by helping you more fully learn and live your faith, helps ensure that you will complete your recovery journey.

In the end, not only will you recover from the emotional, physical, and spiritual trauma of your divorce, you will have a deeper and more vibrant faith. Proving, once again, that God brings good out of all circumstances — even divorce.

> *We know that all things work for good for those who love God, who are called according to his purpose.* - Romans 8:28

CONTENTS OF THE PARTICIPANT KIT

"Divorce is a detour, not a dead end." - Vince Frese

The *Recovering from Divorce* Participant Kit contains these key items that are especially designed to work together to aid in your recovery:

Participant Guide: This book guides you step-by-step through the program. It contains key chapters that will teach you how to use the program including: how to tap into the power of your Catholic faith to accelerate your recovery from divorce, how to use the P-R-A-Y method to ensure your success, and details of the activities for each session.

Divorced. Catholic. Now What? Book: This book has helped thousands worldwide recover from divorce. It is an excellent resource for helping to understand how to meet the challenges of your divorce through your Catholic faith. It is your guidebook, if you will, to recovering from divorce by more fully learning and living your faith.

***Divorced. Catholic. Now What?* Companion Workbook**: This workbook compliments the *Divorced. Catholic. Now What?* book with questions to help you reflect and live what you are learning. It helps you answer the question: "Now what do I do with this information I have learned?" It is essential to applying what you are learning.

***Prayers for Divorced Catholics* Book**: This book is a one-of-a-kind collection of prayers written by a divorced Catholic for divorced Catholics. It provides rosary meditations, stations of the cross reflections, prayers to key saints that want to help you in your recovery, and more. This book is sure to become your "go-to" reference as you more fully embrace your Catholic faith.

Bonus Materials: Included in every kit are additional bonus materials that will help you in your recovery. This can include a rosary, a CD, a book, or other materials.

How to Use the Participant Kit

"Our Lord is walking with you as you go through this program and He wants you to succeed!" - Vince Frese

The *Recovering from Divorce* Program consists of thirteen sessions. There are typically several steps to completing each session. It is important that you set aside time each week to work through the session. The more time you are able to devote each week, the more progress you will make. It is recommended that you allocate an hour each week to read and review the session material and the at least 10 minutes each day praying and reflecting on it. (I will go into that in depth shortly.)

Here is an overview on how to use each component during a session:

***Divorced. Catholic. Now What?* Book**: Each week you are to read the assigned chapter out of this book. Occasionally, a session requires you to read two chapters. It is important that you take the time to read each chapter thoroughly. Feel free to highlight, underline and write in the margins. This book is your reference guide not just to your recovery from divorce, but, also, to your faith. Make it work for you.

Case: Most chapters include a case. A case is a real-life scenario that describes in personal detail the challenges that the chapter is addressing. You will probably relate to the struggles that the people in the case are experiencing.

Core Content: This is the main subject that the chapter is addressing. This material is based on the teachings of our Catholic faith, and there are usually references to Scripture, writings of the Doctors and Saints of the Church, and the Catechism. Plan to really dig in here.

Now What?: This section is designed to give you practical ways to implement what is taught in the chapter. Don't feel like you have to complete each item; however, you should complete at least one of the suggested items. This is how you make real what you are learning.

Meditation: The meditations are a direct connection to Sacred Scripture supporting what has been taught in the chapter. The meditations consist of an opening prayer, a petition (a request to Our Lord to open you mind and heart to what you are going to read, two or three main points from the Scripture — known as "lights" — and a closing prayer. Please take time to read and think and pray about the contents of the meditation. These can be very powerful and transformative.

***Divorced. Catholic. Now What?* Companion Workbook:** This
workbook is designed to help you integrate what you are learning
into your life — to really start to tackle your challenges by living your
faith. Each chapter of the workbook coincides with the chapter in the
book. In these chapters are questions and exercises for you to think
about, prayer about, and, in some cases, wrestle with.

Some of what the Catholic Church teaches is difficult to live, yet,
it is by honestly grappling with these difficult teachings that we
receive the most healing and make the most growth. When you
happen upon a difficult teaching, talk to Our Lord about it. Let Him
know that it is hard and that you really need His grace to live it. Our
Lord is walking with you as you go through this program and He
wants you to succeed!

***Prayers for Divorced Catholics* Book**: As you will learn, prayer is
fundamentally important to your recovery, and to your life as a
Catholic. The *Prayers for Divorced Catholic* book will help, and
encourage, you to pray. The prayers it contains are from the
perspective of a person experiencing divorce and calling out to Our
Lord for help, strength, and support. You receive all these benefits by
praying these prayers. In the chapters on Tapping Into Your Catholic
Faith and The P-R-A-Y System you will learn how to use this prayer
book to its fullest.

The Daily Inspirations: The email Inspirations contain powerful messages that will encourage and inspire you each day of your recovery journey. It is recommended that you subscribe to the Daily Inspirations via email by going to divorcedcatholic.com/daily-inspirations. Start your day every morning by reading the Inspiration you find in your inbox or for that week's session.

Tapping Into Your Catholic Faith

"Your Catholic faith is the key to your recovery from divorce." - Vince Frese

Before my divorce, I was what I would call a "cultural" Catholic. I went to Mass on Sunday because that was how I was raised. I made sure all my kids made their sacraments because I received all of mine. If I prayed, it was only when things were really bad. The rosary was something my mom taught me how to pray when I was a kid and I had not picked it up since. I loved my faith in a nostalgic kind of way, and that was that.

When my divorce hit, my life was thrust into crisis and chaos. Impulsively, I turned to my Catholic faith. Not because I was this strong Catholic, but because I was desperate. I would have tried just about anything at that point if I thought it would help me. The most radical thing I did was start going to daily Mass. Why? Because it was the only thing that brought me peace. At first it was just for a minute or so after I walked in the church door — it felt like a sanctuary. Then, the more I went, the longer the peace lasted, eventually staying with me after I walked out the door. This was the beginning of my odyssey in rediscovering my Catholic faith.

Over the course of the next three to four years, I really dug into my Catholic faith. It was not always easy, or pretty. At times, I struggled mightily with accepting and living some of the teachings of the Church. Sometimes it felt as if I was in a tug-o-war with God. I had just come out of a period of my life that was filled with deceit and lies. I just wanted the truth. You have to be careful what you wish for, you just might get it — and, boy, did I!

With all my struggling, wrestling, and an occasional temper tantrum, God revealed the truth to me. What I discovered was the Catholic Church contains all the wisdom, truth, and guidance necessary to recover from divorce. And, I don't just mean patching up your life and hobbling on. I mean a complete renewal.

Each of us was created for a unique purpose. Sadly, many people think that divorce changes all of that. It doesn't. Living your Catholic faith fully is the way to discover and live your God-given purpose.

Better still, Our Lord wants you to not just trudge through life weighted down by your struggles and scars. He wants you to have an abundant life filled with peace and joy. This doesn't mean that you ignore reality and pretend like your divorce didn't happen, or doesn't really hurt. No, what it means is that by centering your life on your faith, and therefore on Christ, His love defines you, not your divorce — or all the crappy things people have said or done to you.

When this happens, all the bad stuff is external. The peace and joy are internal and can't be taken away, no matter what happens (or doesn't happen) to you.

So, hopefully you are standing up and shouting "I want what you are telling me! I want to reclaim the God-given purpose for my life! I want to live the abundant life of peace and joy that Christ promised me!" Good! This program is all about walking you through the steps necessary to more fully learn and live your Catholic faith, and in the process recover from divorce and reclaim your abundant life.

I didn't create any secret formula, or come up with magic words. I simply have pulled together the truth and wisdom of our two thousand year-old Catholic faith and packaged it in a format that is easy to understand and use. Christ, through the Catholic faith, does all the real work, not me.

Let me outline some of the key aspects of our Catholic faith that, if you are not already doing them, you need to integrate into your life. They are not only essential to recovering from divorce, they are essential to living a life of abundance.

The Eucharist

Contrary to what you might think, or have been told, there is so much more to our Catholic faith than holy water and rosary beads. First, and foremost, is the Eucharist. This is the bread and wine that has been changed into the actual body and blood of Jesus during Mass. It is also known as the Blessed Sacrament or Communion. Whatever you call it, as Catholics, we believe that it is *actually* Jesus made *physically* present to us in the appearance of bread and wine. It is not a symbol or a reminder of Jesus. IT IS JESUS!

This is a huge concept that most people, including many Catholics, struggle to understand and believe. Yet, it is the cornerstone of our Catholic faith, and, as you will come to understand, is the cornerstone to you healing from divorce.

The Eucharist rescued me from my pain and despair and healed me from my divorce. It will do the same for you. It is the "magic bullet" that so many are seeking, and you have it available to you everyday, probably within ten miles or less of where you are sitting. Wow!

I incorporate a lot of Scripture into the *Recovering from Divorce* program. You will read in the Gospels how one of the main things that Jesus did was go around and heal people of their ailments. He restored sight to the blind, he healed the leapers, and He made the mute talk — he even raised people from the dead. People were clamoring just to get close to Him, believing that just touching Him would heal them, and they were right. (Matthew 14:36)

That Jesus you read about in the Gospels is the same Jesus you receive every time you receive the Eucharist. So, if Jesus was able to heal all those people in the Gospels, why can't He heal you? He can!

Here is a connect-the-dot moment for you: by receiving the Eucharist at Mass, or being present in front of the Eucharist, Jesus is physically present to you, just like He was for the people in the Gospels. That same healing power of Christ that was available to all those fortunate people two thousand years ago is available to you today, and everyday, in the Eucharist.

Christ's healing power did not end with His ascension into heaven. No! This is why He gave us the Eucharist, so He could be fully present to us through all time. (Read Chapter 6 of the Gospel of John, it's all spelled out there.) Sadly, so many Catholics don't understand this, or tap into the power of the Eucharist.

> *That same healing power of Christ that was available to all those fortunate people 2,000 years ago is available to you today, and everyday in the Eucharist.*

The Mass

Going to Mass is the most complete way to receive Christ in the

Eucharist. The Mass is so much more powerful an experience than most Catholics realize. To many, it is simply a bunch of rote prayers that you are supposed to say at certain times, along with a lot of standing, sitting, and kneeling. In reality, the Mass is the most powerful witness of God's love that we can experience.

At every Mass we are brought back in time and actually become present to Christ's passion and death on the cross, just as the first apostles were. Through this experience, we are reminded of the sacrifice He made for each one of us, because of His tremendous love. Although we can't see it, during the Mass the angels and saints rejoice with everyone present in the saving power of Christ. It is a time when both heaven and earth touch.

Needless to say, behind what appears to be numbly recited words and actions, is the greatest power of the universe made present to us. (A great book that fully explains the Mass is *The Lamb's Supper* by Scott Hahn.)

What we are given as the result of every Mass is Jesus Himself, His very being in the form of the Eucharist. Not only will witnessing the awesome power of our loving God, and celebrating with the angels and saints, fill your heart with gratitude and your mind with awe, you will get to receive the body of Christ. By receiving the Eucharist, He will become part of you. He will touch you and heal you just like He did the throngs of people that searched and found His healing love so many years ago. (Luke 9:11)

I can't say it enough: the Eucharist is essential to your recovery from divorce. If you scrapped this program and did nothing else but receive the Eucharist frequently, you would be miles ahead of those Catholics who don't take advantage of its tremendous healing power.

Sadly, many divorced Catholics search for healing in a myriad of other ways including other faiths, other relationships, or work, sports, and other pursuits, when the very thing that can help them the most is available to them with what they already have: their Catholic faith.

Tapping in the power of the Eucharist is at the heart of tapping into your Catholic faith. If you wish to tap into this power to recover and heal from your divorce, receive the Eucharist as much as you can — everyday, if possible. Most Catholics are programmed to believe that Mass is on Sunday. If you go to Mass on Sunday, you have met your obligation. This is true; however, in the vast majority of Catholics churches Mass is celebrated every day. This means that you can receive the Eucharist every day.

> *Tapping in the power of the Eucharist is at the heart of tapping into your Catholic faith. If you wish to tap into this power to recover and heal from your divorce, receive the Eucharist as much as you can — everyday, if possible.*

I am recommending that you receive the Eucharist everyday, if you can. It is that important to your recovery. I know that schedules may prevent that from happening; however, I also know that we each make the time for other less important things in our lives like sports, Netflix, and Facebook. Make a strong effort to go to Mass at least once or twice during the week.

There are several websites and apps that will help you find out the Mass times of local Catholic churches. I like the app *Mass Times*. It makes it easy to find the nearest Catholic church and its Mass times wherever I am. They have a companion website, TheCatholicDirectory.com. Unless you are in a rural area, there are usually at least one or two Catholic churches within a ten mile radius of you that offer Masses at various times during the week. This should make it very possible to work an extra Mass or two into your schedule.

Think about this: let's suppose you hurt your knee playing tennis. So you go to the doctor, and he/she prescribes one exercise for you to do to heal your knee. You are told that you must do this exercise at least once a week or you will not recover. You are also told that if you do the exercise more than once a week it will speed your recovery and make your knee even stronger. Better still, the doctor tells you that doing the exercise every day will get you the optimal results.

Even though it would take time out of your schedule, and add some additional hassle into your life, chances are you would make the time to do the exercise every day and receive its benefits. Well, that is what going to Mass and receiving the Eucharist does to aid in your recovery from divorce. Do it!

Prayer and the Eucharist

The other way to tap into the power of the Eucharist is being physically present with it. This can be done one of two ways. The first is simply to walk into any Catholic church and look either on the altar, or near the altar, for a small gold box or door. This is known as a *tabernacle*. Inside the tabernacle is the hosts that have been consecrated during Mass and have become the body of Christ.

On rare occasions the Eucharist will not be present in the tabernacle. Since the tabernacle door is locked, you have no way of knowing if the Eucharist is present just by looking at it. The way to determine if the Eucharist is present is to look for a candle, usually red, burning near the tabernacle. In today's modern age, sometimes the candle is replaced with an electric light. Either way, if you see the candle burning or the light on, the Eucharist is present.

Just as the people in Jesus' time were able to go and find Him to receive His mercy, guidance, love, and healing, you are able to do the same thing when you go into a Catholic church and seek out the Eucharist. You can kneel or sit before the tabernacle. You can talk to Jesus in prayer, or simply be present to Him. In any case, you are receiving the immense graces that being physically present to God, the Creator of the universe, provides.

Eucharistic Adoration

The second way to be in the presence of the Eucharist is when it is displayed on the altar. In this case, the Eucharist is displayed in a frame, known as a monstrance. A monstrance is typically very ornate, and often in the shape of a cross. In the center is the consecrated host that looks very much like what you receive during Mass, only larger so it can be more easily seen. Displaying Christ in the Eucharist on the altar and worshipping Him is known as *Eucharistic adoration*, or, simply, adoration.

While at one time, adoration was very popular, its practice waned during the 20th Century. In the last ten to fifteen years, thankfully, there has been a resurgence of adoration in many parishes. Check the parish bulletin, or call the parish office, to find out when adoration is held.

In some parishes, the Eucharist is exposed on the altar twenty-four hours a day, seven days a week. This is known as *perpetual adoration*. This is extremely convenient because you can be in the presence of Christ whenever it is convenient for you, even in the middle of the night.

Adoration is a deeply spiritual time. You are in the presence of God. Seeing the Eucharist is a concrete reminder that Christ is with you. It is a great time to bring all your worries, all your pain, and all your struggles directly to Christ. Allow His presence to comfort you.

He knows everything that you are going through and He wants to help.

Feel free to worship Our Lord in any number of ways during adoration. Talk to Christ as you would a friend. Pray to Him by reciting any of the typical Catholic prayers, such as the Our Father or Glory Be. Or, simply sit quietly in His presence. While He may not talk to you in an audible way, He will "speak" to your heart. Some people describe this as becoming "aware" of what to do, or just "knowing" how to handle a given situation, after being in adoration.

I recommend that you schedule an hour each week to be in front of the Blessed Sacrament. This is commonly called a *holy hour*. The great thing is, especially with parishes that have perpetual adoration, you can schedule this hour whenever it is most convenient for you. Jesus is always there, waiting for you with loving anticipation of your arrival.

Let this hour be your port in the storm of divorce; the one time each week when you can seek shelter from all of its many challenges. Sit before Our Lord and pour your heart out to Him. Ask for His help, guidance and mercy. He will give it to you. You will find that when you make a holy hour part of your week's routine, you will begin to look forward to it with anticipation. It will rejuvenate you and make you stronger and more connected to Christ and your faith.

Confession

When I was a kid, going to a priest and telling him your sins was called confession. Somewhere along the way, I guess the Church decided to give it a more appealing name and now it is called the Sacrament of Reconciliation. Whatever you call it, for many Catholics, going to confession/reconciliation is more terrifying than a root canal. I was one of those Catholics. Aside from a sporadic visit to reconciliation once every eight to ten years when the guilt finally overwhelmed me, going to confession was not part of my life as a Catholic.

My divorce changed that, but not how I ever expected it. I have already mentioned that my path to fully learning and living my faith was a rocky one. The three or four years after my divorce I was groping in the dark. During this time, I would often stumble upon some aspect of my faith that really helped me. This is exactly what happened to me with confession.

One day, about six months after my divorce, I was sitting in an adoration chapel at a nearby church. (By this point in my recovery I had figured out the power of the Eucharist — thank God!) It was a Saturday afternoon and I did not have the kids that weekend. I was struggling mightily with fully living my faith, particularly chastity. I was feeling defeated and worn out.

There were a couple of other people in the chapel at the time.

Suddenly, several people started coming into the chapel and lining up against the wall. I was not sure what was going on. After a few minutes (and about ten more people), I saw the first person in line open a door and walk in. There was a sign on the door that said, "Confessional." Now I knew what was happening. Saturday afternoon confessions had started.

I had not been to confession in a long time. I sat there trying to ignore the growing line of people. Then I began to notice that as people entered the confessional they tended to have a serious, almost somber, look on their faces. Yet, when they emerged from the confessional, they had a relaxed, peaceful look on their face. Many were even smiling. This got my attention. I wanted the peace that they had. It was then that I decided to get in line.

When I went into the confessional I was very nervous. I am sure my face looked just like those that I saw going in before me. I was not really sure what I was going to say; however, coming up with sins to confess was not a problem. I had a storehouse of those.

When I walked in I was surprised at how young the priest was. I thought, "How could he possibly help me. He is so young, and I am sure he can't relate to the pain of divorce." When I sat down, the priest smiled and nodded hello. Then he said a prayer over me that immediately helped me relax. I anxiously told him that it had been many years since my last confession.

What he said next surprised me. He smiled again and said, "Welcome home." I was not expecting that. I was somewhat expecting a disapproving look; I got just the opposite. Suddenly, I forgot my anxiety. I did feel welcome!

I nervously listed a few of my more benign sins, and then the floodgates opened. I started to spill my guts about how I was really struggling with my life after divorce and all the pain, shame, and hopelessness I was feeling. I told him about how hard it was to live the chaste life that the Church was calling me to live and how unfair it felt since I was not the one that wanted the divorce. I rambled on for quite a while.

When I was done, I was once again expecting some type of chastisement for my many failings. It never came. Instead what came was a very gentle expression of understanding. He told me that Our Lord and all the angels and saints in Heaven rejoice when someone comes to confession. (Luke 15:7) He told me that he could totally relate to the challenges of chastity, as he was called to be chaste as well. This really surprised me. In my nervousness I had forgotten that priests are called to live a chaste life — he really could relate to my struggles.

He then told me something that I was not expecting to hear. He told me that I was carrying a heavy cross in much the same way that Jesus carried His cross. He told me that, while carrying my cross was difficult, I could connect my struggle and suffering to the struggle and suffering my kids were experiencing because of the divorce. By doing this, he told me that I could actually help make their burden easier by "carrying it on my cross." He asked me if I was willing to do that. I said, "Of course!"

One of the biggest sources of pain from my divorce was watching my children suffer. Now this priest was offering me a way to actually use my suffering to make my kids' suffering less painful for them. This was a no-brainer.

I walked into the confessional feeling like I was carrying a thousand pound weight on my back. I walked out of the confessional feeling light as a feather. Not that all my pain and struggles had vanished, but I now had a much better understanding of how to cope with it, and actually help my kids in the process. This blew my mind.

I am sure I had a smile on my face when I emerged from the confessional, just like the others I had seen that day. Ever since that day, confession has been a routine part of my life.

What I have come to realize is that on that day in the confessional, I experienced Christ's mercy in a very real, and very powerful, way. I felt so loved, accepted, and welcomed — just the opposite of how my divorce made me feel. Confession became a sanctuary for me. It was the place that I could go and truly feel the peace that had been wrung out of my life.

This same peace, love, and acceptance are available to you as well. I highly encourage you to take advantage of them. Some people return to confession the same way I did, by simply getting in line. Other people find it less intimidating by making an appointment with the priest. Either way, know that priests understand the courage it takes to come to confession, and are so pleased when people return to this sacrament. You will experience Christ's love and mercy at a time when you need it most. Take advantage of it by going to confession routinely.

Like the Eucharist, receiving the Sacrament of Confession/ Reconciliation is essential to your recovery from divorce. When people ask me how often they should go to confession, I tell them as often as necessary. The more you go, the more you will be sensitized to the sin in your life — the first step toward eliminating it. The more sin you eliminate from your life, the better decisions you will make, and the more peace and joy you will experience. Who doesn't want that?!

In general, going to confession at least once a month is a good habit to form. If you haven't been in a long time, that may seem like a lot. Trust me, once you return to this sacrament regularly you will wonder why you didn't take advantage of it sooner.

The P-R-A-Y Method

"I have simply taken the truth of our Catholic faith and created a method for living it more fully and more routinely." - Vince Frese

In the previous section, I explained how you can tap into your Catholic faith. I went into detail on how the power of your Catholic faith, particularly the sacraments, was vital to your recovery. I also emphasized how forming the habits of receiving the Eucharist and going to confession routinely is key to your healing, and to your life. All great stuff!

As you look over all the parts and pieces of the *Recovering from Divorce Kit*, and think about everything you just learned about tapping the power of your Catholic faith, you may be feeling like you did when you opened a Lego kit for the first time: overwhelmed. I understand. In this section, I am going to give a simple way of putting all these pieces together. I call it the P-R-A-Y method.

Well, isn't that just clever, a faith-based recovery program that uses the acronym of P-R-A-Y! As cute as this may seem, at the heart of this concept is a step-by-step method that will help you integrate your Catholic faith into your life. If you follow this method, you will experience the same healing power of Christ as those that were touched by Him two thousand years ago.

Again, I did not create anything newfangled; I have simply taken the truth of our Catholic faith and created a method for living it more fully and more routinely. The P-R-A-Y method will ensure this.

An Overview of P-R-A-Y

As you have already learned, it is your Catholic faith that is essential to recovering from divorce. When I started on my quest to figure out my life after divorce, I was flailing around in my faith. I wasn't sure how to pray or what to pray. Some days I would pray for more than an hour, other days not at all. I would stumble upon a new teaching in the Catechism and then not pick it up again for a month. Sometimes I would be very successful in living my Catholic faith, sometimes not. I did not have any process for learning or living my faith. I did whatever seemed right. As a result, my progress was erratic.

While my progress might have been erratic, every step I took fanned the flames of my desire to learn what the Catholic Church taught and live it. After a few years, I started to receive spiritual direction from a priest. He helped me to structure my approach. His advice helped me become more purposeful and effective in my faith pursuit. As a result, my progress become much more consistent, and my recovery accelerated.

The P-R-A-Y method is the result of everything I have learned and used over the years. This method is a simple and straightforward way of consistently learning and living your Catholic faith.

Here is an overview of the P-R-A-Y method:

P - **Pray**: As you might expect, prayer is vital to your relationship with Christ and living your faith.

R - **Reflect**: You can't live what you don't know. *Reflect* is learning your faith by reading the program materials, Scripture, and the Catechism.

A - **Act**: As St. James said, "Faith without works is dead." (James 2:26) The Act component is about putting into action what you have learned.

Y - **You**: Like any successful athlete knows, you must take care of your body. The You component is focused on doing the important things to reduce stress and restore peace.

P-R-A-Y in Detail

What I would like to do now is to take each component of the P-R-A-Y method and explain it in detail. This is the method you will use as you go through each session of *Recovering from Divorce*.

<u>Pray</u>

When I was a kid, I was given a prayer book for my First Communion. It seemed to have a prayer for everything, including protection from storms and reducing your time in purgatory! As Catholics we have no shortage of prayers. For me, as I was reengaging my faith, I was not sure what to pray. Should I pray the rosary each day? Should I just talk to Jesus? What about praying to the saints? Often I would feel like I was not "doing it right," and my prayers wouldn't be effective. It all seemed so confusing and intimidating.

It is recommended that you pray everyday. How long? Well, there is no magic formula; however, at least ten minutes a day will help ensure that you are staying spiritually fit and connected to Our Lord and His will. Of course, more is always better. The key is to make it part of your daily routine like you would exercise or taking a shower.

Here is a recommended approach to prayer:

Pray to the Holy Spirit. Christ gave us the Holy Spirit to guide us in His absence. Whenever you pray, it is recommended that you ask the Holy Spirit to lead and guide you in all your thoughts, words and actions. Here is one of my favorite prayers to the Holy Spirit:

Come, Holy Spirit!
Replace the tension within us with a holy relaxation.
Replace the turbulence within us with a sacred calm.
Replace the anxiety within us with a quiet confidence.
Replace the fear within us with a strong faith.
Replace the bitterness within us with the sweetness of grace.
Replace the darkness within us with a gentle light.
Replace the coldness within us with a loving warmth.
Replace the night within us with your light.
Straighten our crookedness, fill our emptiness.
Dull the edge of our pride, sharpen the edge of our humility,
Light the fires of our love, quench the flames of our lust.
Let us see ourselves as you see us
that we may see you as you have promised
and be fortunate according to your word:
"Blessed are the pure of heart for they shall see God (Mt. 5: 8).

Pray one decade of the rosary each day. It is as simple as picking that day's mystery (Joyful on Monday and Saturday, Sorrowful on Tuesday and Friday, Glorious on Wednesday and Sunday, and Luminous on Thursday), and then choosing one of the five mysteries for that day. For example, on Monday you would pick one of the five Joyful mysteries and focus on that event in Christ's life while you pray the ten Hail Marys. The *Prayers for Divorced Catholics* book makes this easy for you as it has a prayer for each mystery of the rosary. See Chapter One in the *Prayers for Divorced Catholics* for a complete explanation on how to pray the rosary and the prayers for all the mysteries.

Have a conversation with Christ each day. This is simply talking to Jesus as if you were sitting across from your best friend at Starbucks. Tell Him what is most pressing on your mind. Let Him know what you are most anxious about, what you fear, and how you feel. Like a good friend, He wants to help you. Ask Him for His help. Ask Him for His advice and counsel. Ask Him for what you need the most. Be sure to take at least a minute or two at the end of your conversation to sit quietly and "listen" for His reply. Most often this comes as a gentle awareness or thought. These are called "lights." This is when having a journal handy is very helpful. Write down what you "heard" during this time of prayer. You don't necessarily have to act on it right away. Having the journal will allow you to look back to see if the there is a pattern or consistency to the lights you are receiving.

Reflect

In our busy lives it seems that we barely have time to get the basic things done like working, eating, and sleeping. And divorce makes it worse, as tasks that were previously split between two people must now all be done by one person. This is especially difficult for single parents as they must now take on all the parenting responsibilities as well. What tends to happen is that no time is left for yourself.

It makes sense that if we don't take time to exercise, our physical body suffers. The same is true for our spiritual well-being. We must take time to feed ourselves spiritually or we become spiritually weak. This affects all aspects of our lives, especially our emotional state, our decision-making, and our ability to be a good role model to others, particularly our children.

The P-R-A-Y method helps ensure that you are reading, learning, and living the important truths of our Catholic faith. Here is what is recommended you reflect on routinely.

Scripture: The Word of God is sacred. It has the power to transform lives. The Gospels are particularly potent as they contain the actual words that Jesus spoke. If you want to know "what would Jesus do," read the Gospels. The Psalms are also especially helpful when struggling with divorce as they are filled with encouraging words on how God loves and helps His people.

Ignorance of Scripture is ignorance of Christ - St. Jerome

If you are not sure what Scripture to read, there are many excellent resources. First, and foremost, are the readings of the Mass. Every Mass contains readings from Scripture including from the Psalms, the Old or New Testament, and the Gospels. Since Mass is celebrated everyday, an excellent way to connect with Scripture daily is to read the readings of the Mass. There are several excellent resources that will help you do this. The Magnificat is a publication you can subscribe to and receive a monthly booklet of all the Mass readings. There are also many online resources including www.usccb.org. There are many Catholic apps as well. I enjoy the Magnificat app, as well as iMissal.

Since the Gospels contain the actual words of Our Lord, Jesus Christ, you are encouraged to read them routinely. There are online resources available that will email you the Gospel reading of the day, along with thoughts on how to understand and live the message of the Gospel. One of my favorites is http://www.regnumchristi.org/en/daily-meditation/

Catechism: The Catechism of the Catholic Church is the primary source of what we believe as Catholics. It is the encyclopedia of our Catholic faith, if you will. In the Catechism you will find detailed explanations on virtually everything we believe as Catholics, why we believe it, and the references to back it up from Scripture, the writings of the early Church fathers and saints, documents for previous Councils of the Church, writing from the popes, and more. It is a virtual treasure trove of our faith. It is the best resource any Catholic has to learn what the Church teaches and why.

As a Catholic experiencing divorce, you are likely to have many questions and uncertainties regarding your faith. The Catechism is your "go to" resource. Since it is a reference guide, you typically don't read it like you would a book (although you certainly could). The

Catechism has an excellent Table of Contents and Index, making it easy to find what you are looking for. These paragraphs are usually of particular interest, and apply in a specific way, to divorced Catholics:

1650-1651: Divorce and remarriage without an annulment

2382-2386: What the Church's teaching is regarding divorce

2337-2359: Dating and intimacy after divorce

If you do not have a Catechism, you can order one at: www.divorcedcatholic.com/books.

Spiritual Reading: Over the years, the Catholic Church has been blessed with an abundance of writers whose works help us to more fully understand and live our faith. You are encouraged to seek out these writings and read them routinely. Most of the most honored saints of the Church are honored because of the contribution to the faith that their writings provide. St. Augustine, St. Therese of Lisieux, St. Teresa of Avila, and St. Faustina, are but a few of the many saints that have shared their deep insights and knowledge.

When there is a particular challenge that faces the Church, it is common for the pope to provide his insights and guidance regarding the issue. This is done by issuing a letter, or encyclical. These can be very helpful in understanding the Church's position, particularly on contemporary issues.

Virtually all of the writings of the saints and the popes can be found online for free.

Program Materials: The *Recovering from Divorce Program* book has compiled all the teachings of the Catholic Church that pertain to the challenges and circumstances unique to divorce. It contains many references to Scripture, the Catechism, and writings of the saints and popes. By reading the material for each section, you will be exposed to all these important writings. The *Program* is so powerful because it applies the teachings of the Church to the specific circumstances of divorce. By reading and digging into this material, you will be given the guidance and wisdom contained in the 2,000 years of the faith to help you navigate your life after divorce. Like the Catechism, the Recovering from Divorce Program book will be a vital reference for you in the future.

Act

The third component of P-R-A-Y is Act. Act is just as it sounds: to do something with what you are learning. Simply reading about what you should do, is not enough. When you promptly use what you have learned, you have a better chance of remembering it and integrating it into your life. There are two ways to help you with this: journaling and a resolution.

Journaling: Something almost magical happens when you write something down: you are more likely to remember it. And when you remember something, you are much more likely to learn from it. Keeping a journal as you go through the Program will help you to remember and apply what you are learning in your life.

Another significant benefit of journaling is it helps you to work through issues and problems. Like an architect who draws up a solution to a particular building problem, your journal is where you can get down on paper all aspects of a problem you are wrestling with. Often, just getting it down on paper makes the problem seem less daunting, and often a solution emerges in the process. Plus, writing down your struggles is a great stress reliever.

Journaling acted as my daily pressure release valve. Whenever I felt the stress and anxiety building, I would get out my journal and write until I felt better. I was free to say anything I wanted, about anybody I chose, and it was only between God and me. This was a tremendous help for me, and it often kept me out of trouble by helping me avoid saying or doing something I might regret.

Journaling is an excellent way to capture any inspirations of the Holy Spirit. As I mentioned in the section on prayer, you want to write down any thoughts, or "lights," that come to you while praying. This is so important. If you don't, you are more likely to miss something important that God is trying to communicate to you.

Journaling is a fundamental part of the *Recovering from Divorce Program*. That is why we include a bound journal. To get the full benefit of the program, plan to start journaling — often.

If you are more of the techie-type, like me, you are certainly welcome to use an electronic journal. Use whatever is more likely to help you journal. I personally use the *Day One* app on my iPad. It is awesome. I even cut and paste the Scripture verses right into my journal. Since my bible (I use the New American Bible translation on the Olive Tree Study Bible app), my missal (iMissal), and my books are all on my iPad, I can easily pull up my journal and type in my lights, thoughts, and ideas as they occur to me.

Resolution: The reason making New Year's resolutions is so popular is because most people have areas in their lives they wish to change or improve. As we all know, making a resolution is one thing, keeping it is another. To change or improve, you must keep your resolutions.

I have found that I am much more likely to keep a resolution if I complete it the same day I make it. To help you live what you are learning in the Program, you will be asked to make — and keep — a resolution. Usually, it involves a resolution to complete for each session; most resolutions can be completed the same day. Some of the resolutions are to be completed each day, like your resolution to pray. Others, just once a week, like a holy hour. Often, you will be asked to make a resolution to help you live the main virtue or teaching contained in a Gospel passage. The more you are able to keep your resolutions, the more progress you will make in your recovery from divorce.

You

The last component is: You. It is vital to your success with this program (and in life, for that matter) that you take care of yourself physically, emotionally, and spiritually. Much of what you learn in the *Program* is from a spiritual perspective; however, I can't stress enough how important it is to take care of yourself physically and emotionally.

Going through a divorce is such an overwhelmingly demanding time. This creates so much stress and anxiety, wreaking havoc on your body and your mind. Another fundamental aspect of your recovery is learning how to relieve the stress you are experiencing. Unless you do that, you will greatly undermine the benefits this program provides.

Exercise: To take of yourself physically, I highly recommend that you incorporate thirty minutes of some type of physical activity into your day. It can be as simple as walking, or as intense as a Zumba class. The key is to get your body moving and your heart rate up. (Of course, if you have any health issues, you will want to consult your doctor before beginning any exercise routine.)

When I was going through my divorce, I took up jogging. I am sure it saved my life. By the end of day, I would be a knot of nerves and stress. By strapping on my running shoes and going for a run through my neighborhood, I would return home much more relaxed. The exercise channeled all the stress out of my body. If I had not found this outlet, I am sure the stress would have given me a heart attack or stroke. Make the time each day to exercise. It is that important.

Find peace: Along with exercising, doing something each day that brings you peace is so important to your recovery. This can be anything from reading a book, listening to music, or picking up a long neglected hobby. It doesn't matter what it is as long as it is healthy and restores peace. Divorce robs you of peace, and you have to be purposeful in restoring it. Certainly your renewed spiritual life will restore peace, especially when you receive the sacraments and pray. It is also important to find temporal channels for peace.

It may be hard to believe that you could ever find peace again. I advise you to start small. Do that one thing each day that gives you even just a minute of peace. If you persist, what you will find is that each day the peace will last a little bit longer than the previous day. Over time, you will find that your activity becomes your oasis in the storm of life after divorce. It is important to give yourself that relief.

For me, it was playing my guitar. I was not very good, but it didn't matter. I was playing for God and me. Usually, I would work to learn one of my favorite Christian songs. It distracted me from the painful realities of my new life after divorce. I would look forward to that twenty to thirty minutes I had after I put the kids down for the night to strum away. After awhile, I would get lost in my guitar playing, and it was not uncommon for me to play for an hour or more without realizing it. This brought much needed peace into my days.

Find something that brings you peace. It will help you endure the daily difficulties of divorce and help in your recovery.

How to Use the P-R-A-Y Method

Now I would like to give you a simple guide to how to use the P-R-A-Y method to help you recover from divorce. The method is straightforward and after a day or two you should be able to readily incorporate P-R-A-Y into your daily routine.

PRAY

Daily:
- Holy Spirit prayer
- One decade of the rosary selecting the mystery based on the day of the week (5 minutes)
- Conversational prayer (5 minutes)

Total Time: ten minutes/day

Bonus:

- Daily Mass (30 minutes)
- Weekly Holy Hour (1 hour)

REFLECT

Daily:
- Read the daily Mass Psalms and Scripture readings (9 minutes)
- Read the day's *Daily Inspiration* (1 minute)

Total Time: ten minutes/day

Weekly:
- Read the Recovering from Divorce Program session materials. (20 minutes)
- Watch the Program video for the session. (10 minutes)

Total Time: 30 minutes/week

Bonus:
- Read spiritual books, writing of the saints, encyclicals from the popes.

ACT

Daily:

- Write in your journal any thoughts or inspirations (lights) you received during prayer and when reading the Mass readings, especially the Gospel.
- As a result of your prayer and reflection, identify an area of your life where you need to change, improve, or incorporate Church teaching and make a resolution to focus on it.

Total Time: 10 minutes/day

Weekly:
- Complete Program workbook session exercises. (20-30 minutes)

Total Time: 30 minutes/week

YOU

Daily:
- Do 30 minutes of exercise. (30 minutes)
- Do an enjoyable activity that brings you peace (10-30 minutes)

Total Time: 40-60 minutes/day

Some of you may be thinking that you don't have the time to complete the P-R-A-Y steps each day. Okay, I hear you. Let's break it down. The Pray, Reflect and Act steps take a total of about 30 minutes a day. The You step is mainly exercise. For those of you that already have an exercise routine, you are only adding an additional 30 minutes of routine activity to your day. For those of you that don't have an exercise routine, you know it is the right thing to do and will have long lasting health and emotional well-being benefits. If anything good can come from your divorce, maybe it just might be your being in better physical shape!

Many of us waste so much time each day. We have so many distractions like TV, Netflix, Facebook, and games on our phones. I bet if you totaled up the amount of time you are spending on these types of activities it would come to at least 30 minutes a day. Isn't cutting back on these less than productive activities to be able to do the few steps that will make a solid, lasting recovery from your divorce worth it? Of course it is!

I promise that if you commit to completing the P-R-A-Y steps each day you will make a full and lasting recovery from your divorce, and you will have a life of faith that will strengthen, guide, and inspire you (and many others) for the rest of your life. And you will reclaim the purpose for which God created you, and live the abundant life He promises.

Participating in a Group

Participating in a group provides unique advantages, including: mutual support and encouragement from others in the group, a camaraderie that exists when a group of people have been through a common experience, and a group of people that you will get to know well and form close friendships.

If this is your first time in a group, it is understandable you may be anxious. What follows will help you understand what to expect during group sessions, the dynamic that forms in a group, and things you can do to make sure you are getting the most out of the group experience. Hopefully, once you are done reading this section, you will feel more comfortable about participating in your group.

The Group Sessions

The group sessions follow a defined format. You can expect the group session to last between 60-90 minutes. Here is how the group meeting time is structured:

5 minutes: Opening Prayers

These prayers are the same prayers you prayed for the session you are reviewing at detailed in the Recovering from Divorce Sessions section of this guide.

5 minutes: Session Overview

Your facilitator will review that week's session. This is mainly a review of the main concepts, and not an in-depth teaching. You will want to make sure you review all the session materials before the group session.

15 minutes: Watch *Voices of Hope* DVD Segment

You will watch a video segment from the Voices of Hope DVD. These videos are from Catholics who, just like you, have experienced divorce. They give their powerful and inspiring testimonies of the healing and hope they found by living their Catholic faith.

45 minutes: Group Discussion

You will be able to share your thoughts and feelings about the session topic with the group. It is through this sharing that you will experience the benefits of a group dynamic. You will come to know that you are not going through this experience alone; others are experiencing many of the same emotions, challenges, and victories. You will hear different perspectives, be encouraged by your group members, and encourage others on their journey to recovery.

5 minutes: Wrap-up/Closing Prayer
The facilitator will recap the group session, announce the session to be covered next, and end the meeting with prayer.

The Group Dynamic

The first time I experienced the therapeutic power of a group meeting was when I was invited to work with my archdiocese to help them better understand the needs of divorced Catholics. I had only been divorced a few years, and I had reached out to my archdiocese with an idea for a divorced Catholic ministry. I was invited to come to a meeting with other divorced Catholics to share my ideas.

On the day of the meeting, I walked into the room and met about ten other divorced Catholics. The woman that was hosting the meeting had a very well planned agenda ready — however, we never got to the agenda! The group, who really didn't even know each other, spent the next hour and a half spontaneously sharing their experience with divorce. The more we shared, the more we bonded. We were all surrounded by people who totally understood what we had been through. It felt like taking a cool drink of water after being lost in the desert. There was such a sense of relief and hope in the room. We had to schedule another meeting to discuss the agenda items!

This is what will happen with you when you attend the group sessions. You will bond with the others in the group over your common experiences with divorce. Our Lord knows that we are not meant to suffer alone; this is why He worked in and through communities while he was on this earth. He still works that way today.

> For where two or three are gathered together in my name, there am I in the midst of them. - Matthew 18:20

Getting the Most Out of the Group Sessions

Here are some guidelines that will help you get the most out of the group sessions:

- **Prepare ahead of time**: Each session will require you to read, pray, and complete some exercises. This will require about an hour each week of your time. Commit to doing this each week. The more you prepare, the more you will benefit from the recovery that the group sessions provide.

- **Be on time**: To maximize the amount of time available to all in the group and to minimize distractions, commit to being on time each week. The meeting will start promptly at the scheduled time.

- **Share your thoughts**: You are encouraged to share openly what is on your heart and mind. Don't worry about being right or wrong. The key is to talk about what you are experiencing, what you are struggling with, what you fear, and what is working for you. You will get so much more out of the group by engaging in the conversation. Don't be afraid to speak your mind, just be respectful to all.

- **Don't monopolize the conversation**: You will want to be respectful of what others have to say and give all a chance to share. It is great if you are not shy and have no problem sharing with the group, just make sure that you are not doing all the talking. The facilitator is there to encourage others to share. Don't feel like you need to fill the silence with conversation.

- **Don't counsel others in the group**: The Holy Spirit is the counselor for the group. This is why the group begins with a prayer to the Holy Spirit. Resist the urge to give direct counseling to other members of the group. It is fine if you share what has worked for you on a given topic, just don't point out people directly and give advice.

- **Don't criticize comments from others**: It is very important that everyone feels open to share. Do not criticize comments made by others. This is not charitable and will stifle the openness of the group. If you disagree with what someone is saying, or have had a different experience, share it by making your comments about you, not the other person. Instead of responding with "I disagree…" you can respond with "When I was faced with that situation, I…"

- **Respect everyone's privacy**: People will not share openly if they believe that what they say will not be held in confidence. For the group to bond, trust must be present. You will deepen the trust of the group by not repeating to others what is shared in the group.

- **Don't spouse-bash:** It is certainly understandable that you are experiencing a great deal of emotion regarding your divorce. That is why you are attending the *Recovering from Divorce* sessions. It is common that much of these emotions are caused by what your former spouse did, or did not, do. Do not openly criticize your former spouse. This takes the focus off of you, and shifts it to someone who is not present, undermining the effectiveness of the group. It is okay to talk about your former spouse's activities, just keep the focus on you, not them.

- **Put into practice what you learn:** The purpose of going through the Recovering from Divorce Program is to help bring about change in your life. Simply reading or talking about something, doesn't help unless you act on it. The more you act on what you are learning, the more effective it will be. Commit to doing the exercises and putting into action what you are learning in the group.

RECOVERING FROM DIVORCE SESSIONS

The pages that follow detail each of the Recovering from Divorce sessions. The P-R-A-Y format is used as this follows the same format that you will use as you complete the session materials at home.

SESSION ONE
PRAYING IN TIMES OF DISTRESS

What You Will Learn:

This session will explain why prayer is fundamental to recovering from divorce, the different types of prayer, and how you can develop a daily prayer life.

Completing this Session:

PRAY:

- Begin with the Prayer to the Holy Spirit:

Come, Holy Spirit!
Replace the tension within us with a holy relaxation.
Replace the turbulence within us with a sacred calm.
Replace the anxiety within us with a quiet confidence.
Replace the fear within us with a strong faith.
Replace the bitterness within us with the sweetness of grace.
Replace the darkness within us with a gentle light.
Replace the coldness within us with a loving warmth.
Replace the night within us with your light.
Straighten our crookedness, fill our emptiness.
Dull the edge of our pride, sharpen the edge of our humility,
Light the fires of our love, quench the flames of our lust.
Let us see ourselves as you see us

that we may see you as you have promised
and be fortunate according to your word:
"Blessed are the pure of heart for they shall see God (Mt. 5: 8).

- Pray the Third Glorious Mystery of the rosary: The Decent of the Holy Spirit, contained in the book, *Prayers for Divorced Catholics.*

REFLECT:
- Read Chapter One of *Divorced. Catholic. Now What?.*
- Read and reflect on the Gospel meditation from Luke 11:9-13 on page 21.
- Read the Daily Inspiration, PERFECT PRAYER (vincefrese.com/perfect-prayer)

ACT:
- Complete the exercises for Chapter One in the *Divorced. Catholic. Now What?* workbook.
- Complete the resolution on page 22 of *Divorced. Catholic. Now What?.*

YOU:
- Make it a point to talk with Christ during your daily exercise time.

SESSION TWO
ANGER WITH OUR SPOUSES, OURSELVES AND GOD

What You Will Learn:

This session will examine anger as a natural emotion associated with divorce, how to recognize the signs of anger, and how to manage anger.

Completing this Session:

PRAY:

- Begin with the Prayer to the Holy Spirit:

   Come, Holy Spirit!
   Replace the tension within us with a holy relaxation.
   Replace the turbulence within us with a sacred calm.
   Replace the anxiety within us with a quiet confidence.
   Replace the fear within us with a strong faith.
   Replace the bitterness within us with the sweetness of grace.
   Replace the darkness within us with a gentle light.
   Replace the coldness within us with a loving warmth.
   Replace the night within us with your light.
   Straighten our crookedness, fill our emptiness.
   Dull the edge of our pride, sharpen the edge of our humility,
   Light the fires of our love, quench the flames of our lust.
   Let us see ourselves as you see us

that we may see you as you have promised
and be fortunate according to your word:
"Blessed are the pure of heart for they shall see God (Mt. 5: 8).

- Pray the First Sorrowful Mystery of the rosary: The Scourging at the Pillar, contained in the book, *Prayers for Divorced Catholics.*

REFLECT:
- Read Chapter Two of *Divorced. Catholic. Now What?.*
- Read and reflect on the Gospel meditation from Matthew 5:38-48 on page 35.
- Read the Daily Inspiration, NORMAL AGAIN (vincefrese.com/normal-again)

ACT:
- Complete the exercises for Chapter Two in the *Divorced. Catholic. Now What?* workbook.
- Complete the resolution on page 37 of *Divorced. Catholic. Now What?.*

YOU:
- Use your daily exercise time to vent your anger by increasing your intensity.

SESSION THREE
WHY DID GOD ALLOW THIS TO HAPPEN?

What You Will Learn:

This session will answer the question: "Why would God allow bad things to happen to people?", examine the concept of free will, and show how God always brings good out of bad situations when we trust Him.

Completing this Session:

PRAY:

* Begin with the Prayer to the Holy Spirit:

  Come, Holy Spirit!
  Replace the tension within us with a holy relaxation.
  Replace the turbulence within us with a sacred calm.
  Replace the anxiety within us with a quiet confidence.
  Replace the fear within us with a strong faith.
  Replace the bitterness within us with the sweetness of grace.
  Replace the darkness within us with a gentle light.
  Replace the coldness within us with a loving warmth.
  Replace the night within us with your light.
  Straighten our crookedness, fill our emptiness.
  Dull the edge of our pride, sharpen the edge of our humility,
  Light the fires of our love, quench the flames of our lust.

Let us see ourselves as you see us
that we may see you as you have promised
and be fortunate according to your word:
"Blessed are the pure of heart for they shall see God (Mt. 5: 8).

- Pray the First Glorious Mystery of the rosary: The Resurrection, contained in the book, *Prayers for Divorced Catholics.*

REFLECT:
- Read Chapter Three of *Divorced. Catholic. Now What?.*
- Read and reflect on the Gospel meditation from Mark 10:46-52 on page 48.
- Read the Daily Inspiration, WHY ME (vincefrese.com/why-me)

ACT:
- Complete the exercises for Chapter Three in the *Divorced. Catholic. Now What?* workbook.
- Complete the resolution on page 50 of *Divorced. Catholic. Now What?.*

YOU:
- Make it a point to use your free will to eat more healthy foods, get more sleep, and avoid excessive alcohol use.

SESSION FOUR
WHAT DOES THE CHURCH REALLY TEACH ABOUT DIVORCE?

What You Will Learn:

This session will examine what the Catholic Church teaches about divorce by understanding what it teaches about marriage and exploring what the Catechism says about divorce.

Completing this Session:

PRAY:

- Begin with the Prayer to the Holy Spirit:

    Come, Holy Spirit!
    Replace the tension within us with a holy relaxation.
    Replace the turbulence within us with a sacred calm.
    Replace the anxiety within us with a quiet confidence.
    Replace the fear within us with a strong faith.
    Replace the bitterness within us with the sweetness of grace.
    Replace the darkness within us with a gentle light.
    Replace the coldness within us with a loving warmth.
    Replace the night within us with your light.
    Straighten our crookedness, fill our emptiness.
    Dull the edge of our pride, sharpen the edge of our humility,
    Light the fires of our love, quench the flames of our lust.
    Let us see ourselves as you see us

that we may see you as you have promised
and be fortunate according to your word:
"Blessed are the pure of heart for they shall see God (Mt. 5: 8).

- Pray the Fourth Joyful Mystery of the rosary: The Presentation, contained in the book, *Prayers for Divorced Catholics*.

REFLECT:
- Read Chapters Four and Five of *Divorced. Catholic. Now What?*.
- Read and reflect on the Gospel meditation from John 11:1-44 on page 65.
- Read the Daily Inspiration, GOT YOUR BACK (vincefrese.com/got-your-back)

ACT:
- Complete the exercises for Chapter Four in the *Divorced. Catholic. Now What?* workbook.
- Complete the resolution on page 68 of *Divorced. Catholic. Now What?*.

YOU:
- Remind yourself the importance of exercise and its long term benefits each time you don't want to keep this commitment.

SESSION FIVE
STAY CLOSE TO THE SACRAMENTS

What You Will Learn:

This session will explain the wonderful gifts of the sacraments and how they are vital to recovering from divorce, particularly the Sacraments of the Eucharist and Confession.

Completing this Session:

PRAY:

* Begin with the Prayer to the Holy Spirit:

Come, Holy Spirit!
Replace the tension within us with a holy relaxation.
Replace the turbulence within us with a sacred calm.
Replace the anxiety within us with a quiet confidence.
Replace the fear within us with a strong faith.
Replace the bitterness within us with the sweetness of grace.
Replace the darkness within us with a gentle light.
Replace the coldness within us with a loving warmth.
Replace the night within us with your light.
Straighten our crookedness, fill our emptiness.
Dull the edge of our pride, sharpen the edge of our humility,
Light the fires of our love, quench the flames of our lust.
Let us see ourselves as you see us

that we may see you as you have promised
and be fortunate according to your word:
"Blessed are the pure of heart for they shall see God (Mt. 5: 8).

- Pray the Fifth Luminous Mystery of the rosary: The Institution of the Eucharist, contained in the book, *Prayers for Divorced Catholics*.

REFLECT:
- Read Chapter Six of *Divorced. Catholic. Now What?*.
- Read and reflect on the Gospel meditation from Matthew 26: 26-29 on page 95.
- Read the Daily Inspiration, INEXHAUSTIBLE (vincefrese.com/inexhaustible)

ACT:
- Complete the exercises for Chapter Six in the *Divorced. Catholic. Now What?* workbook.
- Complete the resolution on page 97 of *Divorced. Catholic. Now What?*.

YOU:
- When you experience the peace that comes from doing the things you enjoy, remember that the peace that comes from confession is many times greater and lasts much longer.

Session Six
Dealing with Your Former Spouse

What You Will Learn:

This session will provide some strategies for successfully dealing with your former spouse. It will also examine the concept of temperaments to help you understand your natural tendencies, and those of your former spouse.

Completing this Session:

PRAY:

*   Begin with the Prayer to the Holy Spirit:

    Come, Holy Spirit!
    Replace the tension within us with a holy relaxation.
    Replace the turbulence within us with a sacred calm.
    Replace the anxiety within us with a quiet confidence.
    Replace the fear within us with a strong faith.
    Replace the bitterness within us with the sweetness of grace.
    Replace the darkness within us with a gentle light.
    Replace the coldness within us with a loving warmth.
    Replace the night within us with your light.
    Straighten our crookedness, fill our emptiness.
    Dull the edge of our pride, sharpen the edge of our humility,
    Light the fires of our love, quench the flames of our lust.

Let us see ourselves as you see us
that we may see you as you have promised
and be fortunate according to your word:
"Blessed are the pure of heart for they shall see God (Mt. 5: 8).

- Pray the First Sorrowful Mystery of the rosary: The Agony in the Garden, contained in the book, *Prayers for Divorced Catholics.*

REFLECT:
- Read Chapter Seven of *Divorced. Catholic. Now What?.*
- Read and reflect on the Gospel meditation from Matthew 14:32-37 on page 113.
- Read the Daily Inspiration, THREE SIMPLE WORDS (vincefrese.com/three-simple-words)

ACT:
- Complete the exercises for Chapter Seven in the *Divorced. Catholic. Now What?* workbook.
- Complete the resolution on page 114 of *Divorced. Catholic. Now What?.*

YOU:
- Each time you struggle to complete your exercise routine, remind yourself that your former spouse struggles just like you do with life after divorce.

SESSION SEVEN
HOW ARE THE CHILDREN?

What You Will Learn:

This session exposes the truth of how children suffer from divorce, its long-term impact on their lives, and some strategies to help them cope with this new reality.

Completing this Session:

PRAY:

- Begin with the Prayer to the Holy Spirit:

Come, Holy Spirit!
Replace the tension within us with a holy relaxation.
Replace the turbulence within us with a sacred calm.
Replace the anxiety within us with a quiet confidence.
Replace the fear within us with a strong faith.
Replace the bitterness within us with the sweetness of grace.
Replace the darkness within us with a gentle light.
Replace the coldness within us with a loving warmth.
Replace the night within us with your light.
Straighten our crookedness, fill our emptiness.
Dull the edge of our pride, sharpen the edge of our humility,
Light the fires of our love, quench the flames of our lust.
Let us see ourselves as you see us

that we may see you as you have promised
and be fortunate according to your word:
"Blessed are the pure of heart for they shall see God (Mt. 5: 8).

- Pray the Second Joyful Mystery of the rosary: The Visitation, contained in the book, *Prayers for Divorced Catholics.*

REFLECT:
- Read Chapter Eight of *Divorced. Catholic. Now What?.*
- Read and reflect on the Gospel meditation from Luke 1:57-66, 80 on page 127.
- Read the Daily Inspiration, POUR OUT MY LOVE (vincefrese.com/pour-out-my-love)

ACT:
- Complete the exercises for Chapter Eight in the *Divorced. Catholic. Now What?* workbook.
- Complete the resolution on page 129 of *Divorced. Catholic. Now What?.*

YOU:
- Each time you struggle to complete your exercise routine, ask Our Lord to allow your suffering to take the place of your children's suffering and ease their burden from divorce.

SESSION EIGHT
OUR OWN SELF-WORTH

What You Will Learn:

This session examines the damage divorce causes to one's self esteem and self-worth, and helps to reaffirm your inherent value by exploring God's unconditional love for you.

Completing this Session:

PRAY:

- Begin with the Prayer to the Holy Spirit:

Come, Holy Spirit!
Replace the tension within us with a holy relaxation.
Replace the turbulence within us with a sacred calm.
Replace the anxiety within us with a quiet confidence.
Replace the fear within us with a strong faith.
Replace the bitterness within us with the sweetness of grace.
Replace the darkness within us with a gentle light.
Replace the coldness within us with a loving warmth.
Replace the night within us with your light.
Straighten our crookedness, fill our emptiness.
Dull the edge of our pride, sharpen the edge of our humility,
Light the fires of our love, quench the flames of our lust.
Let us see ourselves as you see us

that we may see you as you have promised
and be fortunate according to your word:
"Blessed are the pure of heart for they shall see God (Mt. 5: 8).

- Pray the First Luminous Mystery of the rosary: The Baptism of Jesus, contained in the book, *Prayers for Divorced Catholics*.

REFLECT:

- Read Chapters Nine and Ten of *Divorced. Catholic. Now What?*.
- Read and reflect on the Gospel meditation from Matthew 5: 13-16 on page 150.
- Read the Daily Inspiration, PRECIOUS AND GOOD (vincefrese.com/precious-and-good)

ACT:

- Complete the exercises for Chapter Ten in the *Divorced. Catholic. Now What?* workbook.
- Complete the resolution on page 151 of *Divorced. Catholic. Now What?*.

YOU:

- At the end of each exercise session, pat yourself on the back for the physical improvements you have made.

SESSION NINE
THE VALUE OF SUFFERING

What You Will Learn:

This session addresses the challenges of suffering, why God allows it, strategies for dealing with it, and how to use it to help you recover and improve.

Completing this Session:

<u>PRAY:</u>

• Begin with the Prayer to the Holy Spirit:

Come, Holy Spirit!
Replace the tension within us with a holy relaxation.
Replace the turbulence within us with a sacred calm.
Replace the anxiety within us with a quiet confidence.
Replace the fear within us with a strong faith.
Replace the bitterness within us with the sweetness of grace.
Replace the darkness within us with a gentle light.
Replace the coldness within us with a loving warmth.
Replace the night within us with your light.
Straighten our crookedness, fill our emptiness.
Dull the edge of our pride, sharpen the edge of our humility,
Light the fires of our love, quench the flames of our lust.
Let us see ourselves as you see us

that we may see you as you have promised
and be fortunate according to your word:
"Blessed are the pure of heart for they shall see God (Mt. 5: 8).

- Pray the Fourth Sorrowful Mystery of the rosary: The Carrying of the Cross, contained in the book, *Prayers for Divorced Catholics.*

REFLECT:
- Read Chapter Eleven of *Divorced. Catholic. Now What?.*
- Read and reflect on the Gospel meditation from Matthew 8: 23-27 on page 163.
- Read the Daily Inspiration, THE GIFT (vincefrese.com/the-gift)

ACT:
- Complete the exercises for Chapter Eleven in the *Divorced. Catholic. Now What?* workbook.
- Complete the resolution on page 164 of *Divorced. Catholic. Now What?.*

YOU:
- As you go through your day, offer up your sufferings for your kids or family to help ease their suffering from your divorce.

SESSION TEN
WORKING ON FORGIVENESS

What You Will Learn:

This session addresses the difficult challenges of letting go of your marriage and forgiving those that have hurt you.

Completing this Session:

PRAY:

- Begin with the Prayer to the Holy Spirit:

Come, Holy Spirit!
Replace the tension within us with a holy relaxation.
Replace the turbulence within us with a sacred calm.
Replace the anxiety within us with a quiet confidence.
Replace the fear within us with a strong faith.
Replace the bitterness within us with the sweetness of grace.
Replace the darkness within us with a gentle light.
Replace the coldness within us with a loving warmth.
Replace the night within us with your light.
Straighten our crookedness, fill our emptiness.
Dull the edge of our pride, sharpen the edge of our humility,
Light the fires of our love, quench the flames of our lust.
Let us see ourselves as you see us
that we may see you as you have promised

and be fortunate according to your word:
"Blessed are the pure of heart for they shall see God (Mt. 5: 8).

- Pray the Fifth Sorrowful Mystery of the rosary: The Crucifixion, contained in the book, *Prayers for Divorced Catholics.*

REFLECT:

- Read Chapters Twelve and Thirteen of *Divorced. Catholic. Now What?.*
- Read and reflect on the Gospel meditation from Luke 23: 33-34 on page 186.
- Read the Daily Inspiration, FREEDOM (vincefrese.com/freedom)

ACT:

- Complete the exercises for Chapter Thirteen in the *Divorced. Catholic. Now What?* workbook.
- Complete the resolution on page 188 of *Divorced. Catholic. Now What?.*

YOU:

- Practice forgiveness by forgiving yourself when you fail to keep your exercise commitment.

Session Eleven
Sex and Dating as a Divorced Catholic

What You Will Learn:

This session reviews God's design for our sexuality, the pressures to be sexually active, the Church's teaching on chastity, and how to experience the abundant peace and joy that comes with living a life aligned with the truth of our faith.

Completing this Session:

PRAY:

- Begin with the Prayer to the Holy Spirit:

  Come, Holy Spirit!
  Replace the tension within us with a holy relaxation.
  Replace the turbulence within us with a sacred calm.
  Replace the anxiety within us with a quiet confidence.
  Replace the fear within us with a strong faith.
  Replace the bitterness within us with the sweetness of grace.
  Replace the darkness within us with a gentle light.
  Replace the coldness within us with a loving warmth.
  Replace the night within us with your light.
  Straighten our crookedness, fill our emptiness.
  Dull the edge of our pride, sharpen the edge of our humility,
  Light the fires of our love, quench the flames of our lust.

Let us see ourselves as you see us
that we may see you as you have promised
and be fortunate according to your word:
"Blessed are the pure of heart for they shall see God (Mt. 5: 8).

- Pray the Second Glorious Mystery of the rosary: The Ascension of Christ into Heaven, contained in the book, *Prayers for Divorced Catholics.*

REFLECT:
- Read Chapter Fifteen of *Divorced. Catholic. Now What?.*
- Read and reflect on the Gospel meditation from John 4: 3-26 on page 218.
- Read the Daily Inspiration, MEDIEVAL TIMES (vincefrese.com/medieval-times)

ACT:
- Complete the exercises for Chapter Fifteen in the *Divorced. Catholic. Now What?* workbook.
- Complete the resolution on page 221 of *Divorced. Catholic. Now What?.*

YOU:
- Every time you are tempted to not keep your exercise commitment, remind yourself of how good you will feel physically and emotionally when you are finish.

SESSION TWELVE
MARY OUR MOTHER

What You Will Learn:

This session reflects on Mary as our spiritual mother, role model, and comforter.

Completing this Session:

<u>PRAY:</u>

*   Begin with the Prayer to the Holy Spirit:

    Come, Holy Spirit!
    Replace the tension within us with a holy relaxation.
    Replace the turbulence within us with a sacred calm.
    Replace the anxiety within us with a quiet confidence.
    Replace the fear within us with a strong faith.
    Replace the bitterness within us with the sweetness of grace.
    Replace the darkness within us with a gentle light.
    Replace the coldness within us with a loving warmth.
    Replace the night within us with your light.
    Straighten our crookedness, fill our emptiness.
    Dull the edge of our pride, sharpen the edge of our humility,
    Light the fires of our love, quench the flames of our lust.
    Let us see ourselves as you see us
    that we may see you as you have promised
    and be fortunate according to your word:

"Blessed are the pure of heart for they shall see God (Mt. 5: 8).

- Pray the Fifth Glorious Mystery of the rosary: The Crowning of Mary Queen of Heaven, contained in the book, *Prayers for Divorced Catholics.*

REFLECT:
- Read Chapter Sixteen of *Divorced. Catholic. Now What?.*
- Read and reflect on the Gospel meditation from John 19: 25-27 on page 232.
- Read the Daily Inspiration, REENTRY (vincefrese.com/reentry)

ACT:
- Complete the exercises for Chapter Sixteen in the *Divorced. Catholic. Now What?* workbook.
- Complete the resolution on page 233 of *Divorced. Catholic. Now What?.*

YOU:
- Whenever you are suffering physically or emotionally, look to Mary as your role model of fortitude and strength, as she endured walking with her son, Jesus, to His death on the cross.

SESSION THIRTEEN
HOPE FOR THE FUTURE AND OUR VOCATION IN LIFE

What You Will Learn:

This session helps you understand that you were created by God for a special purpose, how your recovery from divorce has given you new experiences and insights to full this purpose, and some strategies for discovering and living this purpose.

Completing this Session:

PRAY:

- Begin with the Prayer to the Holy Spirit:

  Come, Holy Spirit!
  Replace the tension within us with a holy relaxation.
  Replace the turbulence within us with a sacred calm.
  Replace the anxiety within us with a quiet confidence.
  Replace the fear within us with a strong faith.
  Replace the bitterness within us with the sweetness of grace.
  Replace the darkness within us with a gentle light.
  Replace the coldness within us with a loving warmth.
  Replace the night within us with your light.
  Straighten our crookedness, fill our emptiness.
  Dull the edge of our pride, sharpen the edge of our humility,
  Light the fires of our love, quench the flames of our lust.

Let us see ourselves as you see us
that we may see you as you have promised
and be fortunate according to your word:
"Blessed are the pure of heart for they shall see God (Mt. 5: 8).

- Pray the Third Glorious Mystery of the rosary: The Decent of the Holy Spirit, contained in the book, *Prayers for Divorced Catholics.*

REFLECT:

- Read Chapters Fourteen and Seventeen of *Divorced. Catholic. Now What?.*
- Read and reflect on the Gospel meditation from Matthew 13: 44-46 on page 245.
- Read the Daily Inspiration, COUNTERWEIGHT (vincefrese.com/counterweight)

ACT:

- Complete the exercises for Chapter Fourteen and in the *Divorced. Catholic. Now What?* workbook.
- Complete the resolution on page 246 of *Divorced. Catholic. Now What?.*

YOU:

- Each day as you exercise say a special prayer of thanks to Our Lord for your health.

Made in the USA
Columbia, SC
31 December 2020